*A*dversaria

To Frances
In Akron. . . .
In Exeter. . . .

Adversaria

TIMOTHY RUSSELL

TRIQUARTERLY BOOKS
NORTHWESTERN UNIVERSITY PRESS
EVANSTON, ILLINOIS

Northwestern University Press
Evanston, Illinois 60208-4210

Printed in the United States of America

First printing, 1993

Library of Congress Cataloging-in-Publication Data

Russell, Timothy
        Adversaria / Timothy Russell.
              p.   cm.
        "TriQuarterly books."
        ISBN 0-8101-5027-1 (cloth). —ISBN 0-8101-5002-6 (paper)
        I. Title.
    PS3568.U79A64   1993
    811'.54—dc20   93-27870
                                                        CIP

The paper used in this publication meets the minimum requirements of the
American National Standard for Information Sciences—Permanence of Paper
for Printed Library Materials, ANSI Z39.48-1984.

CONTENTS

ACKNOWLEDGMENTS

The poems collected in this volume were first published in the following: *Antietam Review*, "In Bono et Malo"; *Best of 1987* (Ohio Poetry Day Association), "In Personam"; *Best of 1989* (Ohio Poetry Day Association), "In Novus Ordo"; *Black River Review*, "In Ipsissima Verba"; *Cedar Rock*, "In Loco"; *Circumference*, "In Otium"; *5:am*, "In Aegri Somnia"; *Greenfield Review*, "In Adversum," "In Excambio"; *Hill & Valley*, "In Medias Res"; *Kestrel*, "In Absurdo," "In Deliciis"; *Laurel Review*, "In Consideratione Praemissorum," "In Folio"; *Louisville Review*, "In Re"; *Pearl*, "In Aequo Animo," "In Locus Delicti"; *Pennsylvania Review*, "In Gross," "In Medio"; *Raccoon*, "In Linea Recta"; *Venue*, "In Plano"; *West Branch*, "In Alio Loco," "In Deceptio Visus," "In Dubio," "In Embryo," "In Esse," "In Exitu," "In Haec Verba," "In Posse," "In Rem Versum"; *Yarrow*, "In Absentia," "In Damno," "In Propria Persona." Some of these poems also appeared in three chapbooks: *The Possibility of Turning to Salt* (Ohio Poetry Day Association, 1987); *In Dubio* (State Street Press, 1988); and *In Medias Res*, in the anthology of chapbooks, *A Red Shadow of Steel Mills* (Bottom Dog Press, 1991).

Note on the Titles

In the few cases where I have strayed from standard Latin grammar, I have done so knowingly, in a considered way, for a variety of reasons.

IN RE

The thing about this place, in the background,

wherever local scenery goes slack,

between houses snug as teeth, beyond trees,

the patch of corrugation or smokestack,

the glimpsed steel coil or snatch of chain-link fence,

the flinty abundance of railroad track,

the thing all around this place, is the mill.

White petals of the black locust flutter

less like snow or ash than live confetti

to celebrate with summery clutter

some seasonal transition otherwise

veiled from sight. And all we do is mutter

about increased turns on the platers, say,

knowing nothing of what happened today.

IN VADIO

I will show you the oriole nest

it took me until March eleventh to find.

I will show you the maimed sycamore

shriek of a tree that's endured

humiliation all along.

I will show you blue/orange flames

dancing instead of the moon

above the blast furnaces.

I will show you my glass hand

and introduce you to the woman

who lives in a shed with prisms,

if I should recognize her.

I will show you garlic and rose of sharon.

I will show you orange water

reflecting an iron bridge.

I will show you a lagoon.

I will show you the BOP and the FPW

although I cannot take you inside either.

I will show you heaps of slag.

I will show it all to you,

I give you my word.

IN DAMNO

I am still here.

The electric failed last night

when someone fleeing pursuit

crashed on Freedom Way

heading for the bridge.

I suppose suitable news

photographs have been developed.

There were sirens downtown

and people out with flashlights

as if searching for clues.

I went out to look at the mill

which has as I suspected

a separate power source.

I returned to my porch,

smoked in the dark and thought

of lighting some kerosene lamps.

When the lights went out

I suppose the bridge itself

vanished. I am still here

afraid for now to move.

IN DUBIO

Smoke plumes coil in the valley

like cavalry dust, and irises

so purple they must ache bloom

in front of the white block wall,

but rescue is still improbable here

where the moon is as likely

to pass behind heated vapors

rising from a boiler-house stack,

as if it were a lemon slice

sinking in some summer drink,

as it is to catch a locust branch

delicate and vaguely Oriental,

lying across it like scrimshaw,

the same hour, the same night

where cardinals nest in the wisteria,

Baltimore orioles in the sycamore,

and sparrows in the air conditioner,

where fresh asparagus is exotic,

and men tend machinery all night

as if it were troubled livestock.

IN PERSONAM

Mercury vapor drifts through the bedroom

screen along with the mill's concerted whine,

that monotonous lullaby. I lie

awake listening to engines shunting

gondolas at the Walnut Street junction

and thinking the maple leaves must tremble

with the racket glancing off them like light.

Who is at fault for my insomnia?

It is not the man who founded the mill,

nor the engineers and brakemen who let

the cars slam tonight, nor whoever lights

this city with vaporized mercury.

I put my body to this noisy test,

use it at the mill, now wish it would rest.

IN NOVUS ORDO

The Mulkeys all have yoyos

today, and they are casting

tiny planets here and there,

creating another universe,

ignoring the gray drizzle.

By this time next week

another gang of hoodlums

will again be gouging the shiniest cars

in the neighborhood

while the Baltimore oriole

fidgeting among the wet blossoms

in somebody's backyard cherry

ignores them. Maybe it will be

the fifteenth consecutive day of rain.

For now, though, there is hope

sprouting between the bricks

in the Mulkeys' paved playyard,

and certainty springing from the hand

of every Mulkey child. Right now,

this minute, because some prodigal

Mulkey uncle has returned with gifts

for everyone, anything is possible.

IN PROPRIA PERSONA

Patches of locust bloom

like eczema or psoriasis,

whatever my father has on his elbows.

Beyond steeples and stoic roofs,

on the hill called Powerhouse

or Calico,

lush clusters of white flowers

like those on black locusts everywhere

droop no more fragrantly

then they do anywhere,

but those clumps signify

resurgence of forest

where ten years ago

not even grass grew.

The nightmares of falling

from the furnace into some ladle

of fiery slag soup

fade more each week I work

and once-barren hills

nurture new growth:

patches of locust.

IN MEDIAS RES

The ailanthus I found

thriving amid strewn junk

in the abandoned Open Hearth

should not have surprised me,

yet it was somehow lovely

among the cracked trunnions

as it aspired to the latticework

of trusses supporting nothing but sky.

Growing as it did on a steel slab

with nothing beneath but basement

it was vital yet doomed, and still

an ordinary tree of heaven.

IN TESTIMONIUM

It's hard to tell

whether drizzle here

is actually rain.

Both quenchers are idle

but the scrubbers are not

and steam traps hiss all night.

One day last week

cyclone fences

around the parking lots

were icy nets.

It's hard to tell

what's what here.

A salamander is a drum

of burning coke,

holes in it burning orange.

One smokestack is red and white

the others all black

or the color of liver.

Clouds are and are not clouds.

Rain is not always rain.

IN MULTUM

The white dog sleeping on the roof

of the white car sunk to its frame

in front of the peeling yellow house

could be a sign of things to come.

The river was olive drab today

despite glaring sunlight, the window-

pane old enough to have character.

The rusting flagpole wavered.

Later, a spaniel sitting patiently

in the driver's seat of a Bronco,

like somebody's sad, browbeaten mate

stunned with the unfairness of it all,

whatever it all might ever be,

who might have been fantasizing

murder or contemplating money problems

or suicide or even simple flight,

observed me through the steering wheel,

and I thought about imperfections

in the glass, how they are always perfect

no matter what effect they have.

Later still, the white dog barked

from the pinnacle of his empire,

claw marks on the dull finish,

dried splashes of slobber

on the smudged and murky windows,

the heavy collar around his neck hooked

to the chain leading to the wire

stretched above his head,

from the brick porch to the dead tree,

his slowly sinking empire.

IN EMBRYO

"It's a good thing cats don't lay eggs."—*P.K.*

What I want is perfect orange

balanced between yellow and red

neither yet both, like the seed

of bittersweet gathered in winter,

something related to cherry

and at least partly to blister,

to set in front of the window

where the hazy sun behind gauze

would accent the burst cases.

I sold handfuls to the woman

who once gave me a white shirt

for nothing, who fingered her buttons

nervously and laid it on the table,

carefully, as if it were fragile.

The orange I want is glowing

like the tubes in an old radio

maybe tuned to a historic Pittsburgh.

The announcer loves the Pirates.

You can mistake static for the crowd

noises, can almost smell the air,

imagine we're losing in the ninth,

maybe everything depends on Clemente

who may or may not make it to bat.

Or maybe it isn't old baseball,

but the tubes glow, and something stirs,

as if memory were caught in an updraft.

I am sitting in an oaken rocking chair,

one I bought from a widow

who made her living sewing.

For now everything here is quiet,

and I am thinking of an orange tea,

my body aching, twitching, and aging

while something beside tea brews.

If I only had the orange I want,

the solid, glowing orange of molten iron,

something like a toaster's grid,

perhaps I could see the Chinese lanterns

again. It's a good thing cats

don't lay eggs; we might find them clustered

exactly where we least expected them,

say strung out along the baseboard.

They might be some shade of white,

a delicate ivory but with orange yolks.

I am daily getting old, but enjoy the plants

and lately think that if cats did lay eggs,

that would also be a good thing.

I wish you could see the silver maple sway.

IN REM VERSUM

One drink and I wanted to swing

from the hardwood Casablanca fan

but Amos could not find the switch

so jingled some quarters and played

Sinatra on the dusty jukebox

flashing chartreuse and violet.

Kimo snapped his fingers and laughed.

Lenore asked him to please leave

his clothes on this time which he did

until the song of celebration

got the best of him. Our steward

came in as plastic palms shimmied.

Another drink and I forgot time

forgot Marxist implications

of what the press says we have done.

I knew I would go home and sleep.

I was okay when I went in

and asked my wife and her sad friend

to take a bubble bath with me.

Both women laughed when I snapped

my fingers and did my little dance.

IN AEGRI SOMNIA

This heat makes it

almost impossible to sleep,

but easy to say the blast furnaces

north of town make me think

saguaro. Sometimes,

I think I'd rather live

in some more temperate zone,

amid less brutal scenery,

where people are familiar

with public fountains, say,

or jazz at noon saturating

the plaza, small round leaves

quivering in the ornamental trees,

but I know this is weakness.

It is this life that makes

any other life possible.

Blast furnaces actually resemble

the great muscles they are,

huge pipes curving around them

like venae cavae, like aortae.

If it takes a desperate mind

to imagine they resemble saguaros,

then I guess mine is.

IN BONO ET MALO

Except for two dogs,

and the children lolling

about in sleeping bags

in the coolest room upstairs,

we are alone for once

early Saturday morning.

I'm eating toast, and

I crave strawberries.

When I mention this,

she lowers the straps

of her orange nightgown,

and smiles, wickedly.

IN FOLIO

for S.H.

One thing at a time: the blue garage

is set so far into the alley's embankment

its gable roof is an easy step up.

Seven children lie on the gray shingles

like supine corpses in fierce sunlight,

unnaturally still, one still clutching

a stick, another a toy automatic.

It is some kind of drill, I guess,

because they all move at once, as if on cue,

and scramble, yelling, up to the ridge,

and one by one jump to the other side.

It's hard to believe any one of them,

perhaps the blonde with the stick,

could some day foster a tumor

growing like a hive in the rafters,

a tumor that might slowly crack a rib,

like Delbert's first wife, so young.

IN SIMILI MATERIA

When she stopped on the sidewalk,

near the yellow storm drain,

near gnats swarming above the hedge,

the little girl, perhaps three,

yelled something unintelligible

at the doll in the pink carriage.

When she slapped her baby

I remembered flocks of pigeons

erupting from beams and ledges

at the Sinter Plant,

how they would flutter and circle,

flickering in the sun, and always

return to their niches to roost.

IN PLANO

Because hills are not on the maps,

it's easy to get lost here; distant

neighborhoods appear to be adjacent.

A woman asked me today

how to get to Gate #1,

and suddenly I was lost:

Why would anybody

who does not know

where Gate #1 is

want to get there?

The mill of course

is not on the maps.

So I imagined a photograph

my friend said his mother had

of a man and a woman

at the Half Moon farm,

site of the mill's FPW—

twenty-four acres under one roof.

The photograph was taken

after a flood (1936?)

and the man was proud

of the catfish he had caught

in the muck with his pitchfork.

It was as tall as he was.

For a time, I could no more tell

a woman how to get to Gate #1,

though I was headed there myself,

than that catfish could have told

what year it was, or what FPW would mean.

IN ESSE

Houses neat as teeth

run along an opposite ridge

toward a red brick powerhouse.

At sundown they are weird

birds glancing here and there

as they follow their mother

her plumage changing through violet

through purple on its way to indigo.

I saw her struck once

by lurid green lightning

but she absorbed the jolt

swallowed it as it were

easily as a duck would bread.

It was something to see.

IN POSSE

We collect postcards here

from unfamiliar regions

and examine them with some reverence.

We like to think for example

there is a bear somewhere

knee-deep in pure surge and froth

slapping salmon to a pebbly bank

aspen twittering in the background

about the impending feast

under the glossy cobalt sky.

We like to think our bridge transcends

its obvious utility

that its details are significant

the powdery effect of primer

showing through faded aluminum paint

the frayed cable ends

the guardrails nicked and gouged

the grating deck that hums and clanks.

If we were not so busy here

we might travel farther and more often.

IN CONSIDERATIONE PRAEMISSORUM

Seven men sitting on a railroad tie,

ailanthus sprouting like tropical lies

against the blue corrugated sheet iron

behind them, lunch buckets and thermos bottles

open at their feet, all look up at once,

as if by plan. They seem dazed,

or astonished this could happen,

this one open, interminable second.

There is vacancy in their eyes.

They naturally think of home here,

down home, downstate, down "hoopy,"

where they return to hunt or just to touch

the leaves of a familiar bush

or to chase that old emptiness

or to cuss groundhogs or crows

in the corn and come back to tell it,

but right now, this instant,

they all know their break is over.

IN ABSURDO

An old kitchen faucet hangs

on a clothesline hook

screwed into the blue garage,

its thin supply-tubes crimped

like the copper legs

of some chrome bird.

It is not a trophy,

and the paint is blistering.

A can of "federal blue" enamel

dangles in the grimy window,

and a plastic ball floats in the catalpa

like a lost blue planet.

In front, two peonies,

one white, one red,

bloom like political arguments,

each its own perfect example.

IN IPSISSIMA VERBA

I could never explain

how the word *array*

describes the principle

of frond arrangement

in black walnut trees

to anyone in the mill.

Forget the black locusts

erupting here and there

across the strip-mined fields

like mortar explosions.

I'm still working on the swirl

of the weeping willows.

No. You go through the gate

and no matter what time it is

you say "Morning," all day long

knowing maybe you're the only one

who knows you're *in* mourning,

and you call everybody "Uncle,"

and everybody in the mill

has the same middle initial,

which doesn't stand for Francis,

and you tell Uncle Melanie

F. Risovich you love her

and want her to have your babies

so she'll know you're crazy,

and tell Uncle Stephen F. Christian

you love him and want him

to have your babies so all of them

will already know you're crazy

in case you ever find yourself

so unaccountably joyful

you start yammering

about how birds feed or fly

or various aspects of design

you see in different trees

or how you feel like the young girl

you once saw doing one-hand cartwheels

down the middle of Elm Street,

her blonde hair sweeping the asphalt.

The others have left me behind

and taken an excursion to the backcountry

where in-laws are thick as thieves,

so I am here appreciating thirteen trees

in the yard: black scavenger ants

crawling the Norway maple like relatives

waiting for probate, the mimosa's leaves

collapsing every night like tiny governments,

the black walnut and the silver maple

tolerating one another like ordinary neighbors,

three mulberries beneath the tulip

like fruit-stands in the oppressive shade

of a bank building, the American sycamore

shedding leaves and sheets of bark like rags,

the cherry and two wormy plums biding time

like social-security recipients, and the rose

of sharon littering the lawn with torpedo-shaped

blossoms the rubynecks have abandoned.

I've found a pastel portrait my mother did

of me when I was a young boy. God.

IN EXITU

Dusk, mimosa leaves closing like pamphlets,

and the retarded boy wearing black boots

does not see the steps and falls on the low bank

he cannot negotiate, and a yellow flash of oriole

streaks to the pine tree, and a jet leads its vapor trail

glowing against the gray sky, and a woman wearing an orange

scarf and a flowered dress stops to touch a fender,

and the retarded boy's father wheels a bike

down the steps, and the boy takes it by the handlebars

and walks beside it saying, "This is my hot rod," and pulls

the front wheel off the ground, and the bike clanks

when the wheel hits the sidewalk, and the boy takes his bike

around the block, and a robin ventures close enough

to me to inspect me one eye at a time, and flies away,

and the vapor trail slowly dissipates, and the oriole

has flown off somewhere, and the clematis is about to bloom,

not tonight, but maybe tomorrow, and the lady has managed

to disappear, and the yard ornaments designed to amuse

the retarded boy do not move, and the pine tree blends

into the background, and the mercury vapor flickers,

and the retarded boy is not back yet, and I worry,

and his porch light goes on, and the streetlight, too,

and I hear backup alarms from the mill, and ore trains

being shunted at the junction, and I worry.

IN OTIUM

What you do here for entertainment is

you visit the bus station early

to get the Wheeling paper and to see

the latest Little Egypt dressed,

dressed for breakfast, dressed for travel.

She wears her favorite cowboy boots,

and you stare at the sky-blue leather,

the stitching around the stars.

Last night, it was impossible to think

she could be somebody's wife,

somebody's daughter, but today she is,

and her husband is sullen, or surly.

You check the reliable smokestacks

above the hydrochloric-acid plant.

Anyone in town can forecast

what little weather you have.

Picnic tables remind you

of lunchrooms in the mill.

If you don't get up and take a walk

you will go to sleep on the bench,

where ants will explore the fabulous terrain,

calculating how to carry you off.

At night, your porch is bathed

in the purple glow of a bug fryer.

With the radio tuned to the Pirates,

you have another beer.

You have no use for dactyls or iambics.

You visit your sick and bury your dead.

IN PERICULUM

The calliope puffs out clots of steam

behind the marvelous *Delta Queen*,

"The Beer Barrel Polka" echoing across the river,

white splotches hanging briefly in the air

before dissipating like ordinary music,

the paddle wheel slapping and thrashing

water, the wake spreading across the olive surface,

small waves eventually washing over rubble

along both shores. Brightly colored automobiles

of Sunday drivers flit behind the trees

on one bank, and goldfinches flit

through ailanthus on the other.

The delighted passengers gathered around

the shrill contraption, their pastel clothes

shining in sunlight, sing and clap

as the boat thumps its way downstream,

but the boat will barely clear the arching bridge

linking Brown's Island to the east bank.

These passengers on their perilous journey

enjoy themselves, each other, privilege.

Any minute, though, something might rupture.

IN DECEPTIO VISUS

By now, the clapboard siding

on the other side

of this linen-textured wall

is no longer barn-red.

It is maroon in the failing light,

becoming purple. An hour ago

we saw ourselves in this window

pausing to notice where we were

at the time, on the sidewalk,

yet superimposed on the window,

a used-car lot blooming behind us,

thin venetian blinds, open,

behind the glass, this spider plant,

hanging behind the blinds,

and presumably, the rest of the room

behind the plant, but really,

just a sense of depth

we thought must be a room.

Now we have moved inside,

and used cars are over there,

across the street where they belong,

for now, and we are here,

at this table, with coffee,

the surface of mine giving off vapors

we assume are coffee,

and wobbling gently

with some minute movement

of the universe which is otherwise

undetectable, except

for the spider plant shimmering

slightly, which lets us know

the building itself is shaking.

When did you first notice

the goldfish swimming

in the lighted tank across the room?

I want to tell you it could be

heavy traffic somewhere nearby

slowly shaking the whole town down.

It could be the steel mill,

which is the reason for the traffic.

Had we examined our reflection

more closely, we might have seen

that plume of smoke, there, curling toward us.

IN LINEA RECTA

"Rattle of contents is acceptable in this type of merchandise."

1959 was a pivotal year

for Ruth and Charlie.

They already had four boys,

and though they didn't know it yet,

Ruth was finally pregnant with Theresa.

Charlie had a new job,

a promotion, from the mill

to the old General Office.

In December, they bought a new house

two miles away. They loaded

their new, aqua-and-white station wagon,

made fifty trips up two hills,

their furniture always in danger

of sliding out.

       How was I to know,

riding on that green tailgate,

a purple dresser wanting to push

me to the blurred asphalt

running away from my feet,

that in a quarter of a century,

I would be sitting at a window

remembering that warm December day

when I was eight years old

and trying to understand what happened,

how that practically innocent boy

came to inherit a steel mill

thumping in his chest like a heart attack?

IN LOCO

The aluminum girl on the lawn

will not look up from her aluminum book

to admire pink windows at dawn.

She ignores weather, traffic splashing by,

pedestrians, even the bronze night sky

flashing with industrial fire.

She has never seen the oak tree

full of brown and curled leaves like birds

that always seem ready to flee.

She wears a blouse without sleeves

and a peasant skirt. She is barefoot

because it will always be summer.

She has never turned a page

and has no idea she's a statue.

IN EXCAMBIO

Blue/orange flames arrive at dusk
to roost above the blast furnaces
north of town like large birds
flaunting their litmus plumage.
After I had sat a while at midnight
with coffee on the back porch
trying to assess the drizzle,
lights at the Walnut Street junction
casting an amber glow on the mist,
I realized the BOP looms
larger than most cathedrals.

The fiery birds flutter and preen
off and on like recurring dreams.
I went to sleep knowing summer
was going south for the winter
even woke up cold once or twice
dreaming of rituals and worship,

priests wearing cobalt lenses

so they could peer into the vessel

and magical birds who vanish

against the pale sky at dawn.

IN GROSS

This could happen anywhere

this smell in the air

like ozone and cordite

this industrial musk

and this cup of coffee

steaming like a wound

or this sound of glass

like a whiskey bottle

spinning on asphalt

this ticking sound

of beetles at the light

all of it anywhere

but this woman sitting

on this green glider

with paint flaking off

this woman about to speak

this woman only here.

IN HAEC VERBA

Red and white midgets practice

formations and blocking assignments

in the outfield. There are railroad cars

beyond the fence—some SOUTHERN boxes

filled with kitchen cabinets

on the lumber company siding

three anonymous black tankers

on the black iron bridge with the silvery

green willow swirling up behind it

like an all-purpose prayer.

A CHESSIE SYSTEM black cat looks on.

There is a necklace of maroon CR hoppers

almost bulging with ore pellets

about the color of dried blood

strung along the bottom of the hill

presiding over the entire scene

like a judge passing sentence.

There is withered chicory in the wire.

IN DELICIIS

When Violet spells *laundry*,

I hope she never hears it

used in a sentence

the way my mother did.

I daydream, smelling *watermelon*,

noticing the lighted clock,

but time itself is lost.

We are here in limbo, waiting.

When Ivan spells *barricade*,

I think he already knows

something will come between us

in a few short years.

At the end of every round,

there is polite applause

masking the sounds of *exodus*

thudding a murmuring rumor

across the gymnasium floor.

Clusters of siblings and parents

in the *amber* varnished bleachers

thin out like vegetation

at the edge of a desert:

time-lapse photography.

Words fly like indoor airplanes

old men design

to prolong slow-motion flight

beneath an *ornate*, vaulted dome,

but Violet, in corduroy, brings me back

with *stagecoach*, and I think

about old movie heroes.

I hear the word *scarecrow*

and imagine one shouldering a large bird

like a pirate with his parrot.

When Ivan spells *chimpanzee*,

six of the fittest still survive,

half a dozen children remaining

to cast their spells on the judges.

There is a lull in the competition.

Violet is at the microphone.

She frets, having never seen

the word *deacon* before,

and moments later, when Ivan stalls

on the word *escalator*

I mutter my own words: *incarcerate*,

which has fluttered around me

like a monarch these twenty years,

always just out of reach,

waiting for the right moment to land,

and *prophetic*.

IN ADVERSUM

For forty-five minutes I told

my foreman lies about my brother

Wallace—how after half a lifetime

of trying, Wally finally managed

to get himself struck by lightning

on a sunny day, like a poet,

and how Wally dropped everything

climbed into his old green Buick

and headed downstate to find

a thirty-foot walnut log, how

blue exhaust twirled behind him

like a tornado lying down on the job,

and how he brought the log back,

and how he unloaded it in his yard,

and how he carved his totem

although he'd never done much

of anything with tools before,

and how he got me and half

his neighbors to struggle with it,

like ants with a grasshopper leg,

until his wife finally took over

and we got the thing planted for him—

for forty-five minutes I went on,

holding Bogeyman Frank at bay

while I was supposed to be painting

a cage, a wire-mesh cage. I was proud

because he asked me if it was true.

It would be I said,

if I had a brother named Wallace.

Paint the damned cage he said.

IN DIEM

Although it was warm for October

seventeenth his field jacket

(olive drab) (and paint-speckled)

is slung over his shoulder because

there was frost this morning

and thick fog near the river.

Greeting his wife in their garden

he sets his black lunchbox down

among fallen silver maple leaves.

She has a colander filled with broccoli.

One of their children comes to help

gather the last of the black walnuts,

searching two clumps of pale peonies

for the mottled green pods.

There is Swiss chard and one tomato.

The man follows the woman and the boy

to the house, stooping for a leaf rake

he leaves at the door, where he turns

out of habit to check the sky:

a few white clouds sailing overhead.

IN VIVO

Tonight I briefly thought I might explode

In blossom: Once it startled me to think

My blood could circulate a lethal code

Or I could somehow die without a wink

To signal quick return, but now I know

How tenuous my hold is on this life.

(You think you know the scarlet river's flow

Requires its secrecy; you love your wife.)

Until a cure is found for my disease—

So many esses I cannot say it—

Some simple serum, say, derived from peas,

Enough pain accepted will delay it.

Let blood sustain its damaging rumor;

Let me maintain this droll sense of humor.

IN JUDICIO

I admit I saw the woman

that night across Main Street

from the creche (four shepherds,

some sheep—one black—

three kings, two camels—

one saddled with a pack,

so obviously one missing—

an angel wired awry,

a mule, a cow, some straw,

and that nuclear family).

There were white rags

tied to wires like upside-down doves.

This woman had an umbrella

but it was not raining.

Behind the stable scene,

there were soggy flowers

in front of the purple granite memorial.

A squad car stopped traffic

while an ambulance started

for the nearest hospital.

A streetlight flickered out,

then flickered back on.

I spoke to the woman,

and she to me, about weather.

She closed her umbrella.

When she left, she said something

about "flu weather" and "nutrolls."

I stopped in the library

for an address, which I got,

and Fatima accused me of quiet

when I left a few minutes later.

I did not go straight home.

I saw bare light bulbs

through flimsy bedroom curtains.

I saw two white wreaths made of plastic

sandwich bags. I found

a dark blue hat with a yellow logo

on the pavement. It was drenched

and gritty. I hung it

on somebody's chain-link fence.

It was the night of the geminid

meteor showers. But there were clouds.

It was too warm for snow,

too warm to smell coal smoke.

As I left the library,

I saw the aluminum girl

reclining on the lawn,

and her tree still full of brown leaves.

There was some activity

beside the fire department,

pine trees for sale, I think.

One of the doors—the left one—

had a decorated tree painted on it.

The station was lit up,

but I did not go there.

I did not see the woman again.

She was not wearing such dark lipstick

that night. I saw a coffeepot

being put in a window

above Sunday's sermon's topic:

ANGELS. I had to squint to read it.

I remembered Poyner's poem "The Acolyte,"

the angels in it transformed into animals.

More traffic splashed by.

I carried a green notebook.

I guess I am guilty of something.

Still feverish or not, I wake up thinking

the green dial is a luminous city

floating beneath its stereo-light moon—

a tenuous indication of strength at best.

This is flu season. The rainy piano

has stopped for technical reasons, yet

the set receives the nearly silent broadcast.

Outside in the yard, the palimpsest

of trampled snow slowly disintegrates,

holes in it growing like some virus.

I have already reached for the toggle

that will banish this city in crisis

when two flutes tentatively begin.

IN ALIO LOCO

In the next town south

(always another place)

there is a young woman

(young or not, always a woman)

who lives in a shed

(another place again).

Beneath the skylight

cut in the ceiling

she has placed a mirror

flat on her table

on which she examines

a ruby brooch

as if it were a cluster

of red stars in the blue sky.

I will send a message

to her tonight. I will

walk down Purdy Lane

with a hand-shaped bottle

I've been keeping for this.

I will sneak behind

the yellow brick church

cross the parking lot again

asphalt glistening under mercury

vapor. I will follow

the outfield fence

toward the swirling willow

rising up beside the iron

railroad bridge.

I will find Harmon Creek

and drop my glass hand

into water that always flows

water that cannot freeze

my glass hand holding

this message that will

somehow reach the young

woman living alone in her shed.

If you are the woman

I doubt you'd have me

which is not the point.

If you are the woman

who lives in a shed

I want to apologize

for blue/orange flames

atop the blast furnaces

and for the orange water

flowing in Harmon Creek

that can never freeze.

IN ABSENTIA

Trudging up two hundred stairs

as if I knew what to expect

atop an idle blast furnace

I have come to see something.

This is what?

This is what I have?

This is what I have come to?

This is what I have come to see:

Ice particles streaming

out of swirling fog

form small white beards

on the yellow handrails.

I think of magnetism.

And there is nothing in the world

beside this small phenomenon

to notice, frost, not ice.

It happens often.

Last night near here

I saw a light behind louvers

and slowly twirling fan blades.

As far as I know

this could be a ship

on which I am alone.

I think of brevity.

IN LOCUS DELICTI

Frozen grass crunched underfoot.

The polar breeze was important:

a thousand plastic grocery bags

filled with air and possibility

drifted through the neighborhood,

rolling gently and bouncing

across the streets and yards,

cellophane tumbleweeds bumping along

toward the next county.

Bare hedges snagged a few.

Others roosted in the lower branches

of ornamental trees, like fruit,

some wonderful winter fruit.

Or they might have been a virus.

So much depends on state of mind.

IN AEQUO ANIMO

Later, when it's over,

when you are waiting

for the light to change

at the Market Street Bridge,

although it defies reason

to wait at two in the morning

on this deserted stretch,

after your sleep

has been interrupted

by the telephone

and you have answered

your mother's summons

and driven through snow

to your childhood home,

after you have crept

down squeaking stairs

into the gray cellar

you still think of as yours,

and showed your own father

how to relight the pilot light

to his own furnace,

and you have come back up,

and had a cup of coffee,

while you waited with your mother

for the house to warm up,

later, when either way

you are halfway home,

and a red traffic light

in the middle of nowhere

vanishes, and the green

suddenly appears,

you calmly understand

this was a dry run.

IN MEDIO

I don't notice missing fingers

anymore. I don't mention absence

at the knuckle. Details always vary

but there's no point in asking.

Gary smashed his ring finger

against a wall with a buster handle

for example then years later married

a Korean woman who divorced him.

You don't visit somebody's house and ask

why the phone doesn't ring. If only

my shadow had not once slid over her

in the grass beside a fountain

it might not have loomed on her wall.

I tell you I still see the guttering

candle on her dresser. I knew drifts

out back were shrinking in the rain.

It's tempting to say we need rain

to feed rust or to suppress the smell

of creosote and we need to make steel

for rust to feed upon. It's tempting

to shrug and to leave it at that. Lying

perfectly still I heard tiny lightning

crackling in her hair as she flung

her sweater to the chair and danced

her jeans-dance briefly against

the backlit flowered curtains. She

was a butterfly with stunted wings

when she unfastened her bra. I'm sorry

I know less now than I did then

but it can't be helped. You know

I get the feeling I'm being followed

by a silent but relentless glacier.

Sometimes I feel its breath on my neck.

Or I can hear grasshoppers flicking

their legs inside a three-pound coffee can.

I still remember how Robert sewed them together

how long his grasshopper necklace kicked.

Look there. It's swinging upside down

to get at the mulberries only seven blocks

from our fully integrated steel mill.

Long live that male blue jay! Look.

That car wants to swallow the man

pouring water into its radiator.

I've been looking at myself. Somewhere

near here a woman sits with her cat.

She will soon wake up smelling odors

that worry her. I remember small leaves

like patches of brown skin pasted

to wet glass. I remember water seeping

into footprints. Just outside Cincinnati

I saw a pair of Cape buffalo mating.

I see mufflers strewn like torsos

along the highways. I know raccoons

and possums lick the salty asphalt

in spring. I saw sludge slopping

out of clam buckets. Now that I've slipped

over the edge I'm anxious.

Haven't you noticed the change? I know

I should eat less and quit smoking.

I saw myself on a window. The man

asleep atop the made bed wore khaki pants.

He slept in the attitude of a prisoner

as if he were listening to faint murmuring

in the hollow of his elbow. I saw

a girl taunting her brother. Her hair

was a blonde flag her brother aimed at.

I believe he wanted to stone her to death.

I think the world is on fire. I saw

a sweatbees' nest—eight carcasses

oblivious to intrusion—and the one

living resident zipped at my wrist.

I sawed a four-by-four and exposed

white and nibbling larvae of some sort

suffering shock. I found a hollow pile

of feathers and bones where a pigeon

was dismantled by ants. It happens.

I must make arrangements I guess

I've seen wondrous fish with gills sucking

thin air. I've seen wondrous birds

blown up like rags against the sky.

I've slept under a galvanized roof

ignoring hornets conferring in the rafters

while it rained. I've seen circular leaves

sprouted overnight in a tulip tree.

I collapsed in a blue wheelbarrow.

I've waited and waited and waited

at the windows of dead flies

in several dilapidated stations

my skeleton emerging at an increasing rate.

Treading water is not so simple.

I hope I see forsythia cascading again.

If I lose a foot or a finger in the mill

if the roof collapses

if nothing happens again or still

if the mirror breaks

if anything and/or whatever

then so be it. Life's too short.

IN ACTU

Looking back now, I arranged everything:

thirty tracks glinting in the amber light

shed by three high-voltage clusters

perching brightly atop their standards

to illuminate the empty railyard,

and the fringe of forest slipping down

the hill. I knew black bricks formed

jagged black letters on the stack

above the unused incinerator

like separate faces on a totem.

The name of the town had to be there.

The lagoon had to be there behind

the silhouette of bunched trees rising

to escort Harmon Creek away from

the lumber company buildings painted orange,

past the ballfield and its dugouts

behind Kroger's and the Ford dealership.

It was night and streetlights

had to be strung out like constellations

in all the declining neighborhoods.

Two plumes rose and merged

above the hydrochloric-acid plant,

and traffic thumped across the Lee

Avenue railroad bridge, headlight beams

briefly flashing up to escape the planet

before the jolt yanked them back.

The long low buildings, of course,

had to be there, black even in daylight,

lying south to north as if magnetically

aligned. I live beyond them.

I know there is a powerhouse above me now

squatting like a duck on the brow of this hill.

I have seen it from my back porch.

I have seen it struck by lightning.

I have seen it turning purple at sunset.

I have seen it and its green aura at night.

It has to be there as surely as the mermaid

bottle has to be on the dining room windowsill,

just above the Christmas cactus.

In five seconds of climbing though,

it's all gone: the four blast furnaces

standing north of town with pipes

wrapping down around them like aortae,

pigeons that had to roost

by the hundreds at the Open Hearth

and the Sinter Plant,

and the BOP flashing like a brain.

In five seconds the fluorescent

red white and blue gasoline signs

flicker one last time in memory,

then I am gone, climbing this hill

toward the powerhouse on Calico,

then all of it below me, behind me,

vanishes. Everything disappears—

until somebody else who lives there,

or works there, on the railroads, say,

comes along to retrieve it.

IN BONIS DEFUNCTI

Sewn behind the circular patch

embroidered SPACE FOR RENT

on the brow of his yellow golf cap

this message folded inside

a paper crane:

If what I have written

in my own hand

had been origami

it would have been considered

lovely and miraculous:

the blue/orange flames

roosting at night

instead of the moon

above the blast furnaces,

like birds with litmus plumage,

miraculous and lovely.

IN NUCE

Had you wanted apples

the mill would not be here.

This would still be orchard.

IN INTEGRUM

I've put my white shirt on

to celebrate my neighbor's glaring roof,

the brick chimney leaning against its own shadow,

the nest of black branches above it all

dissolving into brilliance.

I've put my white shirt on

to celebrate cookies on a plate downstairs

and the pears and oranges in a bowl

with one perfectly curved banana.

I am celebrating the Christmas cactus

blooming in March.

I am celebrating nothing.

I am celebrating today.

I've put a white shirt on.